S0-ARD-922

A Literature/Social Studies Program

Journey to Jo'burg

by Beverley Naidoo

Project Authors:

David C. King

Sharon Flitterman-King

The purchase of this material entitles the
teacher to reproduce student activity pages for
classroom use only. Any other use requires
written permission from Sundance Publishing.

Copyright © 1995 Sundance Publishing
234 Taylor Street, P.O. Box 1326
Littleton, MA 01460

ISBN 1-88741-116-9
10 9 8 7 6 5 4 3 2 DSV

All rights reserved.

Table of Contents

Student Activities

Resource Activity   Skill

1	Study Guide 1	Guiding Reading and Discussion
2	Study Guide 2	Guiding Reading and Discussion
3	Time Line	Ordering Events
4	Map	Locating Places

Inquiry Activity   Skill

1	What the Government Says	Prereading
2	The Sound of English	Vocabulary
3	Glossary	Vocabulary
4	Journey to Selfhood	Book Theme
5	A Student's Account	Social Studies Theme
6	A Fitting End	Social Studies Theme
7	A Story for Freedom	Critical-Creative Thinking
8	Why Do We Care Now?	Critical-Creative Thinking
9	Singing Free	Writing
10	The Next Act	Writing
11	Who's Who in South Africa	Project
12	No Easy Answer	Making Connections
13	Decisions	Making Connections

Copyright © Sundance

Rationale and Description

The connections between the peoples and nations of the world are becoming increasingly more apparent—economically, politically, technologically, and ecologically. If students are to become effective citizens and humane individuals, they must develop a sense of connectedness to humanity, a global perspective that encompasses an awareness of the human strivings common to all peoples, and the desire and skills to solve the problems facing not only their own country but also the world. In addition to acquiring specific information, students need to learn how to structure and use this information—thereby creating knowledge through the process of involvement.

Students learn by making connections. As they develop an information base in history and the other social studies, students connect previously learned information to new information. **CONNECT/Social Studies,** a literature-based program, provides these connections. This program uses the best in children's and young adult historical literature to bring alive a period of history. The historical novel—rich in imagery, characterization, plot, and theme—is an ideal vehicle to make indelible the culture and history of a particular time. Students combine the literary experience and the factual information to make connections among people, history, and their own lives.

CONNECT/Social Studies reinforces the major strands of the social studies curriculum—history, geography, culture, values, government, citizenship, economics. As students read the novel, participate in dialogue, and complete the activities, they will process information, investigate issues, make decisions, think critically, and participate in the political process. As students reinforce and apply these skills and processes, they will also integrate social studies with other areas of the curriculum: they will make more connections.

Each **CONNECT/Social Studies** package contains a Teacher's Guide and reproducible student activity sheets. The Teacher's Guide provides ideas and information that make teaching the program a manageable, effective, and rewarding experience for teachers and students. It gives background on the history, geography, and culture as it relates to the specific book. Teachers may choose to share this information with their students before, during, or after reading the novel.

The Book Synopsis reviews the main events of the novel and summarizes both the literary and social studies themes of the book. The Teacher's Guide also suggests strategies for discussing the literature, with the goal of promoting inquiry and dialogue. In addition, the Links and Curriculum Tie-Ins offer ways to link the book to other topics, themes, or studies in social studies and in other curriculum areas. Each guide also includes a bulletin board idea and a suggested reading list for students and teachers.

The reproducible student activities are designed to help students understand the novel and relate its meaning to their own lives. Four Resource Activities are included in each **CONNECT/Social Studies** package—two study guides, a time line, and an outline map. These activities guide the reading and discussion process and allow students to locate the story in time and space.

The Inquiry Activities encourage interactive learning through discussion, writing, and research. Each activity draws on the literary and social studies experience suggested by the book but also has a specific focus.

- Prereading—provides a way to introduce the novel and social studies content in order to connect students' prior knowledge to the book
- Vocabulary—focuses on the acquisition and application of the vocabulary that is specific to the book or expands upon it
- Book Theme—helps students to recognize and understand an important literary theme
- Social Studies Theme—reinforces a content-area skill or theme that is related to the novel
- Critical-Creative Thinking—provides practice in any of a number of thinking skills and processes (e.g., making observations, predicting, determining cause and effect, making inferences, evaluating information, solving problems, comparing and contrasting)
- Writing—requires students to respond to the book's literary and/or social studies content
- Project—suggests any of a variety of assignments related to the theme of the book (e.g., to conduct research, prepare an oral or a written report, conduct a survey, plan a display, complete a craft)
- Making Connections—requires students to integrate and synthesize the facts and concepts they have acquired during the unit and **connect** them to their own lives

CONNECT/Social Studies is designed for flexible classroom use. Although the reading of the book and the completion of the activities can be assigned to individual students, the literature-social studies experience will be greatly enriched when students work together in small groups or as a total class to conduct a dialogue about the issues and share the results of their inquiries. Whichever way teachers use **CONNECT/Social Studies,** their students will participate in a literature program that builds social studies and global literacy and prepares them for their role as participatory citizens.

Copyright © Sundance

Learning Web

SOCIAL STUDIES

- Arranging events in chronological order
- Reading a map
- Analyzing government statements
- Forming hypotheses
- Comparing literary and eyewitness accounts
- Completing a research project
- Identifying a nation's leaders
- Taking a stand on an issue
- Comparing racial conflict in two cultures
- Recognizing the importance of historical perspective

LANGUAGE ARTS

- Analyzing a novelist's technique
- Identifying idioms
- Analyzing character development
- Comparing fictional and factual accounts
- Drawing inferences
- Writing a persuasive argument
- Researching
- Writing a poem
- Analyzing opposing viewpoints
- Analyzing literary treatments of prejudice

Journey to Jo'burg

MUSIC

- Appreciating the rhythms of South African music

SCIENCE/ SOCIAL STUDIES

- Researching diseases of malnutrition

SPORTS

- Researching the politics of international sports

Copyright © Sundance

Content Background

History

On June 16, 1976, 20,000 black South African students marched toward Orlando Stadium in the township of Soweto, South Africa. They planned to hold a rally to protest a new government law making Afrikaans (an offshoot of Dutch) the official language of instruction in mathematics, geography, history, and social studies. Since the vast majority of students spoke English and/or one of the Bantu languages, they interpreted the new law as a thinly veiled attempt by the white government to discourage Africans from gaining an education. Already angered by the poor quality of education they were receiving in the all-black schools, the students decided to take a stand against apartheid.

Near the stadium, the students were met by a large force of South African police who opened fire and claimed later that they were provoked by stone-throwing students. Two students were shot and killed. The incident touched off a wave of protest and police violence that left 1,000 dead and more than 5,000 injured, and produced hundreds of arrests over the next few months.

The Soweto uprising plays a prominent role in *Journey to Jo'burg*. The roots of that event run deep into South Africa's history, and the event itself continues to cast a long shadow over the country today. An understanding of the struggle against apartheid in South Africa requires some knowledge of its historical and cultural context, much as an understanding of the civil rights movement in this country during the 1960s and 1970s rests on an awareness of what came before and what has followed.

Milestones in South African History

The Dutch established Cape Colony in 1652 as a refreshment station to provide food and fresh water to Dutch trading ships on their long journey to and from the East Indies. The first small band of settlers were all employees of the Dutch East Indies Company. Unable to provision the ships on their own, the company's representatives carried on a lively trade with the peoples that had populated the region for centuries.

In 1657, the government opened the doors of the colony to employees and settlers who wanted to own land and become citizens. These settlers were called Boers—a Dutch word meaning "farmers." The Boers considered themselves God's chosen people. They steadfastly believed that it was God's will that whites should rule over blacks. Using the rationale that black people were inferior to justify their actions, the Boer settlers began importing slaves from all over Africa to keep their homes and work their farms.

It soon became clear to the local African peoples that the Boers meant to stay and that their numbers were growing. Inevitably, cultural friction and competition for land developed between the expanding Boers and the indigenous peoples. Over and over again the Dutch, with their superior firepower, pushed the native population farther and farther into the northern desert regions or into territories too small to support their people.

In 1814, the British took over Cape Colony. Over the next 20 years, they made English the official language of the colony, abolished slavery, and passed laws that set limits on the types of punishment masters were allowed to inflict on their servants. The Boers were outraged. To escape British interference, they began loading their wagons and leaving Cape Colony. During the 1830s, about 10,000 Boers made this move, known as the Great Trek. They marched north and northeast from Cape Town.

The Boers were met with significant resistance throughout their move. In Natal, the Zulus organized a massive offensive against the Boers but were ultimately no match for Dutch guns. The English eventually took

Copyright © Sundance

control of Natal, but the Boers (or Afrikaners as they came to be known) did establish two independent republics called Transvaal and the Orange Free State. In these two republics, black people were not allowed to become citizens, vote, own land, or travel without a pass.

The British accepted the two Boer republics, but any hope of peaceful coexistence between the Afrikaners and the British was shattered when diamonds and gold were discovered in the two Boer republics. Land that the British had once considered of little value now became an enormous source of wealth. The British began looking for an excuse that would allow them to retake control of Transvaal and the Orange Free State. Though it was not their immediate goal, the British were about to take the first step toward unifying South Africa into one nation.

As news of the diamond and gold discoveries spread, the Boer republics were flooded by an influx of immigrants—the majority of whom were British. The Boers resented these "outlanders" and sought to limit their power by denying them the right to vote. The outlanders reacted angrily. Cecil Rhodes, the British governor of Cape Colony, saw an opportunity to use the outlanders' unhappiness as a springboard for throwing the Boers from power. In 1895, the outlander revolt that Rhodes had anticipated did not arise, but the seeds of rebellion had been planted.

In 1899, the Boers demanded that British troops stationed along their borders be removed. When the British refused, the Boers attacked. The result was the Boer War (1899 to 1902), the last of the great wars in Great Britain's imperial history. There was much sympathy for the underdog Boers throughout the world, especially in the United States, but they had little chance against the superior resources of the British.

The treaty of 1902 sought to appease the Boers. The British promised the Boers self-rule as soon as possible and made no attempt to change the status of blacks living in the Boer republics.

The British then combined the British and Boer colonies into the Union of South Africa. A constitution written in 1910 limited the vote to whites; since the Boers, or Afrikaners, were a majority of the white population, they controlled the government. In 1931, the Union of South Africa was granted full independence from Britain.

With the wealth from gold and diamonds, South Africa rapidly became a modern industrial nation. At first, Zulu farmers retained some of their autonomy by providing food for the growing mining and factory towns. But a variety of factors pushed more and more black South Africans to work in the mines, where they received meager wages and poor treatment. Despite the increasing hardships blacks faced in the white-controlled state, even the more liberal British had no intention of letting blacks or other nonwhites participate in the government.

Through the first half of this century, though, many people harbored a hope that black people would be granted their rights and be integrated into the society as participating citizens. But the majority of whites were opposed to any steps toward integration. They were afraid of losing their power to the black majority and justified the continued separation of races on both economic and religious grounds. In 1948, the National Party came to power by promising a policy of apartheid—separateness and segregation—in order to preserve a "pure white race." "Integration," the party said, would be "national suicide."

African opposition to white domination has been continuous throughout this century. In 1902, blacks formed the African National Congress (ANC) to work for peaceful and gradual change. Typically protests have followed an African tradition of nonviolence. As early as 1913, for instance, the black women of the Orange Free State refused to carry passes; when the jails overflowed, the government backed down. And in more recent times,

Copyright © Sundance

two important black South African leaders—Zulu chief Albert Luthuli in 1960 and Archbishop Desmond Tutu in 1988—were awarded the Nobel Peace Prize for their nonviolent protests.

Following the establishment of apartheid as its official government policy, the white South African government became more and more oppressive. In the late 1940s and the early 1950s, the government passed numerous laws to strengthen apartheid and viciously crushed any opposition. As repression increased, so did black resistance. Nelson Mandela, of the African National Congress, and other African leaders began moving closer to a policy of violence. "Fifty years of nonviolence," Mandela said, "have brought the African people nothing but more and more repressive legislation."

From 1948 to 1978, protests—marches, pass burnings, strikes, and work stoppages, as well as occasional bombings of symbols of white supremacy—became more common and more widespread. The government crackdowns became increasingly harsh. Frightened whites, fearing revolution, armed themselves. At Sharpeville in 1960, a protest march ended when police killed 67 marchers—the majority of them shot in the back as they fled. In 1964, the African National Congress was outlawed, and Mandela and several other leaders were sentenced to life imprisonment. From that time, thousands of black South African protesters were jailed without trials.

The Soweto uprising in 1976 was a dramatic example of government repression. The entire world was horrified by images of the police beating and shooting young children. However, the courage of those children to resist had an impact on the older generation of Africans, making them rethink their own reactions to white dominance.

A Time of Changes

In 1978, when Pieter W. Botha became prime minister, the government claimed that it was working toward a solution satisfying to all the groups. Other steps were taken during the 1980s to grant blacks greater freedom of movement and other basic rights. The leaders, however, denounced the reforms, saying that they were only an effort to buy off black anger by giving a few benefits to the small black middle class. Most outside observers agreed that the Botha government did little to lower the walls of apartheid.

As the 1980s came to an end, South Africa continued to seethe with unrest. As Percy Ooboza, editor of the *Johannesburg Post*, put it, "Under the relatively peaceful surface, there is a volcano of anger and discontent. It is only a matter of time until the volcano will erupt." In January 1989, after a minor stroke, Botha resigned, turning over the post to his Minister of Education, F. W. de Klerk. The election of F. W. de Klerk as state president in September 1989 gave many people hope. At his inauguration, he promised to ease tensions and move the country into a new era. One sign of his commitment to this progress was the unbanning of the African National Congress (ANC) and the release of political prisoners, among them Walter Sisulu, 77, former secretary general of the ANC, who had been in prison for 26 years and Nelson Mandela, who had been in prison for 27 years. The sudden political freedom caused an upgrowth of black political parties, including the formation of the Inkatha movement, a Zulu contingent.

In a move perceived as radical by many of his supporters, de Klerk then proceeded to overturn apartheid's significant platforms. In June of 1991, public schools became integrated on a limited basis, public spaces were desegregated, and the Population Registration Act, which many considered the linchpin of apartheid, was repealed. Although the end of apartheid had long been promised by white leadership, de Klerk's reforms were the long-awaited definitive denunciation of apartheid.

Copyright © Sundance

In 1990, as the pillars of apartheid were beginning to come down, Mandela and de Klerk began designing a new constitution for South Africa. Their negotiations were hindered by opposition from extreme groups against the compromises made by Mandela and de Klerk. By 1992, opposition had solidified into equally militant black and white supremacist movements. At one extreme, there was the Afrikaner Resistance Movement, which staunchly resisted the end of apartheid and any change in the status of black people. At the other extreme was the Inkatha party, which distrusted all white political interests and resented Mandela's growing power. In the middle ground were Mandela's ANC and de Klerk's National Party. Even between these so-called moderates, old tensions vented themselves in sporadic violence.

As the national elections neared, grievances among rival political groups had not been resolved. In early 1994, the Inkatha party and the Afrikaner Resistance Movement both threatened to secede from South Africa. Violence erupted between the Inkatha and the ANC causing many white South Africans to doubt whether a black party could govern effectively. Despite the turmoil, on April 28, 1994, the first free presidential election was held in South Africa. Voter turnout was monumental. Mandela had won a landslide victory in an election that international monitors agreed was democratic. The ANC had a cabinet majority with twelve seats, in contrast to the National Party's four seats and the Inkatha's one seat.

On May 10, 1994, Mandela was inaugurated as president of South Africa. Since then, he has made courageous steps toward remedying the enormous disparities of living standards between black and white South Africans. Touring the country after his inauguration, Mandela promised a million new houses within five years, ten years' free education for every child, electricity for millions of homes, and hundreds of thousands of new jobs. Although far behind initial pledges to build new houses and provide educational grants, there is finally peace in South Africa. Hope has improved life for the majority of black South Africans.

Culture

The policy of apartheid was built on and strengthened by long-standing racial divisions within South Africa. Although the situation has improved under Mandela's leadership, divisions and tensions based on race and class remain. The population of South Africa is divided into four racial groups: whites—4.5 million or 16.2 percent; blacks—19.8 million or 71.5 percent; coloureds (primarily people of mixed black and white heritage and Indians)—2.6 million or 9.4 percent; Asians (also considered coloured)—8 million or 2.9 percent. These percentages have been changing in ways that frighten the white minority. The percentage of whites in the population has been declining, while the percentage of black South Africans has been increasing steadily.

Cultural traditions have tended to strengthen not only racial divisions but also divisions within each group. Among whites, for example, the lines between Afrikaners and English are gradually blurring in terms of wealth and position, but intermarriage between the two remains uncommon. In the past, social institutions were separate. English children went to English language schools and joined the Boy Scouts or the Girl Scouts; Afrikaner children attended Afrikaner schools and joined the Voortrekkers. The same division existed in adult clubs and churches.

Coloured people have historically been in a difficult position. Prior to the introduction of apartheid in 1948, they had been sympathetic with the Afrikaners and had hoped to be accepted by the white population. But apartheid policies stripped them of their few economic, political, and social gains, and in the 1950s, many of the younger coloured people began to identify themselves with the Africans.

Copyright © Sundance

The Indian minority that makes up the remainder of coloured people has been a closed population since early in the century when both India and South Africa banned further immigration. The vast majority live in Natal, primarily in towns and cities. While there is a large Indian middle class, there is also a good deal of poverty. There has always been some tension between blacks and Indians. But in recent years, the younger generation of Indians has tended to identify with the black South Africans.

In order to discourage greater unity, white governments of the past consistently emphasized the cultural differences among the black majority. There are also real cultural differences. For instance, there are several distinct language groups, making communication between members of different groups difficult. Customs and history also differ, leading to friction that occasionally exploded into violence. Many of these cultural divisions seem to be disappearing, especially among black South Africans who are living in urban areas.

Wealth—or the lack of it—also divides black South Africans. The vast majority live in abject poverty, locked in a constant struggle against hunger, malnutrition, and disease. In contrast, there is a small middle class that lives comfortably and has been encouraged by government policy to separate from the majority of black people. Even in the Mandela era, class differences divide black interests.

Despite the differences between and within black, Indian, and coloured groups, the groups became increasingly united against whites by the oppression of apartheid. A 1981 report by the Study Commission on U.S. Policy Toward Southern Africa concluded that ". . . increasingly, for all its multiplicity of racial and ethnic identities, South Africa drifts toward polarization: black versus white." This polarization is something that even dissolution of apartheid has not completely corrected. Residual attitudes of fear and mistrust remain, especially between black and white South Africans. This attitude has manifested itself in "white flight"; many white families, afraid of the new political system, have opted to leave South Africa rather than live with the changes.

Glossary

To make *Journey to Jo'burg* sound more authentic, Beverley Naidoo uses South African words and phrases instead of English ones. The following glossary of terms may be helpful as a reference and for clarity when reading *Journey to Jo'burg*.

Baas—Boss, in the Afrikaans language

Hou jou bek—Shut up, in the Afrikaans language

Mielie—Corn on the cob, in the Afrikaans language

Mma—Mother, in the Tswana language

Mmangwane—Little mother, in the Tswana Language

Pap—Porridge made from cornmeal, in the Afrikaans language

Pass—Every black South African over sixteen years of age must carry a passbook at all times. It names the places where the person lives and works.

Rra—Father, in the Tswana language. This is also used by children to be polite to an older person.

Sala sentle—Stay well. This is an expression of farewell in the Tswana language.

Tsamaya sentle—Go well. This is an expression of farewell in the Tswana language.

Copyright © Sundance

Geography

Although the situation is changing, the geography of South Africa has been dominated by apartheid. Where a person lives and works, and even the freedom to move (as *Journey to Jo'burg* illustrates in such dramatic terms), were for decades dictated by government policy.

Historically, white people controlled all of South Africa except for the ten homelands designated for blacks. In the past, the homelands were home to over 70% of the population but accounted for only 13% of the nation's territory. As one might expect, the homelands were located on undesirable lands, too small and too poor to become economically self-sufficient. Because the homelands provided no economic opportunity, workers had to leave them on a regular basis to find work in white areas.

The white South African economy could not have survived without black workers. As Elaine Pascoe writes in *South Africa*, "The homelands policy simply provided a mechanism through which blacks could be denied political rights and through which those whose labor was not required could be kept out of the way." Consequently, even though they had independent homelands, blacks continued to work in the factories, mines, and households of white, urban society. At any given time, only about half of all black South Africans were in their designated homelands. The rest were away for months or years at a time at their jobs. They lived in black townships and shantytowns that existed outside every important South African city. At the time *Journey to Jo'burg* was written, about half the population of Johannesburg lived in the all-black ghetto of Soweto. In order to control black movement, the government mandated that black South Africans carry passes. To many black South Africans, the passbook became the ultimate symbol of white tyranny. Before the system was abolished, tens of thousands of blacks were arrested or harassed annually for failure to produce a pass.

South Africa has the potential to provide a high standard of living for all its people. The country has ample farmland, a pleasant climate, and an abundance of natural resources—gold, diamonds, platinum, manganese, and uranium. With its strong industrial economy, the nation ranks as one of the world's richest countries. Apartheid had limited the enjoyment of these resources to the white minority and a handful of others. Even with black leadership and the breakdown of homelands and segregation, redistribution of wealth will be gradual. Today the white minority remains many times wealthier than the black majority.

Copyright © Sundance

Book Synopsis

Journey to Jo'burg is a story of a young girl's journey of discovery—the discovery of what it means to be black in a rigidly segregated society dominated by a white minority. The journey begins when Naledi and her younger brother Tiro set out for Johannesburg from their home in the northern portion of the country. They must find their mother because their baby sister Dineo is gravely ill and only Mma will know what to do.

Naledi begins the trip with a child's innocence. She has no idea of the distance she must travel—either in the physical or metaphorical sense. During their trip, the two children are befriended by other black South Africans who warn them of the dangers they face outside their homeland. Gradually, often painfully, Naledi learns what apartheid is about: separate buses for whites and blacks; fine homes on tree-lined streets for whites only; and brutal police roundups of black people who are not carrying their passbooks.

Naledi and her brother find Mma and return home with her. At the hospital where Mma takes the baby, Naledi finds out about the poverty and despair experienced by many of her people.

On the journey, Naledi also learns that some young black South Africans have refused to accept apartheid. A new friend named Grace tells her about the Soweto uprising in 1976, when peaceful student protesters were tear-gassed and shot by South African police. The government's use of violence makes black South Africans like Grace determined to break the chains of apartheid.

The novel ends with Naledi's growing awareness of her world and her choices. Dineo is recovering, but Mma fears that she may fall ill again because the family still cannot afford the necessary food. As she lies in bed, Naledi decides that she will seek out students at her school who, like Grace, want to build a better life for themselves and their people.

Links

Journey to Jo'burg presents a variety of topics that can be linked to various curriculum areas. Here are a few suggestions:

- Examine the nature of prejudice in several societies, using sources from literature and social studies.

- Compare apartheid to racial segregation in the United States before the civil rights movement.

- Use current news sources to find out how black South African society is changing since apartheid has ended.

- Study the history of South Africa and the foundations of apartheid as government policy.

- Read excerpts from South African literature of protest—the novels of Alan Paton and the writings of black leaders such as Archbishop Tutu and Nelson Mandela.

- Find out about the role of United States business in South Africa and the policy of the United States toward that country.

- Have students listen to music such as *San Goma*, a recording by Miriam Makeba of songs that recall her South African childhood.

- Research another country where in the present or the past one section of the population has been persecuted by another. What did the oppressed people suffer? What did they do to fight back?

- Research the diseases that result from malnutrition. If it is true that Dineo was sick because she did not get enough milk, fruit, and vegetables, what diseases might she have had?

Copyright © Sundance

Teaching Suggestions and Answers

> This section presents teaching strategies, directions, and suggested answers for each of the student resource activities and inquiry activities. A variety of materials and activities is included so teachers can select those that fit the needs and interests of their students.
>
> The activities and materials are designed for flexible classroom use. Although the reading of the book and the completion of the activities can be assigned to individual students, the literature-social studies experience will be greatly enhanced when students work together in small groups or as a total class to conduct a dialogue about the issues and share the results of their inquiries.

Resource Activity 1 • Study Guide 1

Guiding Reading and Discussion

Before they begin reading, students should review the questions on the first study guide. The guide should be used to focus students' attention on select elements in the novel, thus preparing them for the Inquiry Activities that follow. The study guide may be completed individually or in pairs by students. The Questions for Discussion are especially effective when students consider them individually first and then share their responses in a group. Although they can be used to monitor reading progress, the guides are best used as a study aid, rather than as assessment. The first guide covers Chapter 1 through Chapter 7.

To Think About As You Read

Students' answers will vary but could include the following: **1.** Tiro and Naledi might go hungry, get lost, not be able to find their Mma, be kidnapped, or be arrested. **2.** Naledi and Tiro don't have the money to take their sister to the doctor. Because they don't have the money for a bus ticket, they have to walk to Jo'burg. They don't have much food at their house—their friends give them sweet potatoes and oranges. The pavement burns their feet because they don't have shoes. Their mother has to work in faraway Johannesburg to support the family. They have never seen electric lights before. **3.** Black South Africans share food, rides, advice, and information. The boy in the orange grove, the truck driver, and Grace all help protect Naledi and Tiro from dangers on their journey to find Mma.

Words to Look For

Most of these words are defined in the glossary in the back of the book. *Mmangwane*—respectful term for a female elder; *mielie*—Afrikaans word for corn; *Sala sentle*—stay well; similar to good-bye. *pap*—cornmeal porridge; *Tsamaya sentle*—go well; similar to good-bye; *Tswana*—Naledi and Tiro's language; *Rra*—father, respectful term for a male elder; *baas*—Afrikaans word for boss; *Soweto*—black township located outside Johannesburg

Questions for Discussion

1. Nalede and Tiro sing. Students should understand that the singing is a way for the children to pass the time and to feel more secure about traveling so far from the village. Students' entertainments will vary. **2.** Now that their father has died and is not able to provide income, the family faces greater financial burdens. Because Mma must now work away to support the family, Naledi and Tiro are growing up without any parents. **3.** Students' responses will vary but should include getting caught without a pass, getting flogged for stealing food, going hungry or shelterless. Students should acknowledge that the trip to Johannesburg is a major undertaking for the children. **4.** Grace is outspoken about the problems of life for black South Africans, while Mma quietly accepts them. **5.** In the cities, there are crowds and public transportation. Naledi and Tiro are awed by the luxurious homes of whites. They experience indoor running water and electric lights for the first time. They are surprised that Mma has her own room. **6.** Madam is callous about Mma's request and threatens to get a new maid if Mma does not return in a week. To Madam, a party is more important than Mma's dying child.

Resource Activity 2 • Study Guide 2

Guiding Reading and Discussion

This study guide covers Chapters 8–15. The first half of the book concentrates on all the

Copyright © Sundance

hurdles Naledi and Tiro must overcome to reach Jo'burg safely. The second half of the book focuses more explicitly on the hardships that black South Africans faced every day under the policy of apartheid. As she becomes increasingly aware of her circumstances, Naledi begins thinking of the choices that others have made and the choices that she must eventually make.

To Think About as You Read

1. Black South Africans feared being arrested for not carrying a pass. Many risked losing their jobs if their personal lives forced them to leave Johannesburg for a few days. **2.** Students' responses will vary but should acknowledge that the feelings between black and white South Africans were those of fear, suspicion, and prejudice. **3.** Students' responses will vary. You may want to frame a class discussion around their ideas.

Words to Look For

raid—a sudden attack; *pass*—a book that gives basic information about its carrier. For many black South Africans, the pass was the ultimate symbol of white tyranny; *Hou jou bek*—Afrikaans expression meaning "Keep quiet"; *rubbish*—garbage; *dustbins*—garbage cans; *queue*—a line of people

Questions for Discussion

1. Grace is responding to the injustices in the way black and white South Africans live. Although many black South Africans worked all day cooking and cleaning, they had barely enough food to eat and had to wash themselves at outdoor taps, or faucets. **2.** Grace uses the phrase "time of fire" to describe the violence and anger surrounding the anti-apartheid protests of the 1970s and 1980s. Students may be interested to know that in July 1985 the violence associated with protests became so extreme that a National State of Emergency was declared. **3.** Grace thinks that school is a waste of time because all that schools teach black children is how to be servants. Mma thinks education is very important to have a good life. She is working hard to save enough money for Naledi and Tiro to go to school. **4.** Mma may have been worried that eventually Naledi or Tiro might risk being killed or arrested marching against apartheid. **5.** Mma still cannot afford the medical care and foods that will keep Dineo healthy. **6.** Students' responses will vary.

Resource Activity 3 • Time Line

Arranging events in chronological order

Resource Activity 3 can be used to help students place the novel's events within the history of apartheid in South Africa. The time line begins in 1948 when apartheid became official government policy and extends to the period immediately following the conclusion of the story. The activity sheet asks students to draw the dates for five events from a summary paragraph and enter them on the time line.

Students may use newspapers or magazines to learn about the current situation in South Africa. Students then extend their time line by choosing two recent events that they believe to be significant. Students should write a sentence or two explaining why they believe their events are important in the continuing story.

Suggested Answers

1. 1980 **2.** 1976 **3.** 1960 **4.** 1980 **5.** 1989 **6.** Students' choices and reasons will vary but may include the election of F. W. de Klerk in 1989, the release of Nelson Mandela and the unbanning of the ANC in February 1990, the formation of the Inkatha party in 1990, the dismantling of apartheid legislation in 1991, political tensions between the ANC and the Inkatha party in 1994, and the inauguration of Nelson Mandela in May 1994. Students' reasons will vary.

Resource Activity 4 • Map

Reading a map

One of the pillars of apartheid was the homelands policy that confined black South Africans to certain locations, which they could not leave without a pass. The government's plan had been to make all these homelands independent. But according to the government, when Africans in a homeland accepted independent status, they surrendered all claim to rights in the nation of South Africa.

This map activity will develop students' awareness of how homelands added to the plight of the nation's black majority. The goal of the activity is not for students to learn precisely where each of the ten homelands was located but rather to see the geographic pattern of apartheid and to consider how that pattern precipitated conflict. Although the homelands policy is no longer in existence, because they lack the land or money to move elsewhere, many black South Africans are still

Copyright © Sundance

concentrated in the same areas. The activity will provide good practice in interpreting a map.

Distribute the activity sheets and have students work on the questions individually or in pairs. Go over the answers in class. Then use these questions in a class discussion: Which group did the homelands policy benefit? Why? Suppose a black leader tried to unite all Africans and wanted to speak to leaders of the homelands. What difficulties would he or she face? Students should understand that the white minority benefited from the homelands policy, which kept black South Africans divided and easier to control. Requiring passes when traveling outside the homeland was another way whites controlled the movements of blacks. The geographical separation of the homelands made communication among black leaders more difficult.

Suggested Answers

1. Namibia, Botswana, Zimbabwe, Mozambique, Swaziland **2.** Indian, Atlantic **3.** 10 **4.** Xhosa, Tswana, Ciskei, Venda **5.** three: Tswana, Xhosa, Zulu **6.** Tswana

Inquiry Activity 1 • What the Government Says

Prereading

Developing hypotheses

How you introduce the novel will depend in part on what background knowledge or awareness your students bring to the subject. Many will have heard of apartheid. If the class has not studied apartheid, a simple and useful way to begin is to make a quick inventory of what the students do know. In discussion, or as a brainstorming exercise, ask students what they know, think they know, or want to know about South Africa and apartheid.

Distribute Inquiry Activity 1 and have students work individually. Explain that in South Africa the word *African* is used to describe black people; it is similar to our words *black* and *African American*. In South Africa, people of black and white parentage are referred to as coloureds.

Emphasize that there are no right or wrong answers in this activity. Most students will agree that life under such a government would not be pleasant or easy. Some students may want to talk about similarities with the history of blacks in America. This discussion is a useful way for students to make connections and to foster global consciousness.

Suggested Answers

Students' ideas will vary.

Inquiry Activity 2 • The Sound of English

Vocabulary

Identifying British idioms

Journey to Jo'burg is written in English, but it also contains words from both the Afrikaans and Tswana languages. In addition, spoken English in South Africa is usually British rather than American. This activity will make students aware of the variety in the English language and will call attention to some British idioms.

Explain to the class what an idiom is—a speech form that is particular to a given place or region. Brainstorm with students a list of idioms they are familiar with. For example, in some parts of the country people say "soda"; in others, "pop."

Because she was raised in South Africa, Beverley Naidoo writes in British English rather than American English. The activity sheet has four British idioms. Have the students guess what each word means from its context, find the British definition (most dictionaries will have it), and rewrite the sentence using the American equivalent. The class may enjoy thinking of other familiar British idioms like *chips* for *french fries* and *lift* for *elevator*.

Suggested Answers

1. a motor truck; truck **2.** to move along as if by rolling; moved, crept, rolled **3.** trash or garbage cans **4.** a line or file of people

Inquiry Activity 3 • Glossary

Vocabulary

Using and compiling a glossary

Explain to students that a glossary is used as a reference for words or phrases that might be confusing within a story. Ask students to imagine why Beverley Naidoo chose to use South African words and phrases in her story instead of their English equivalents. Discuss how her decision to include these expressions lends the story authenticity.

Suggested Answers

Students' answers will vary.

Copyright © Sundance

Inquiry Activity 4 • Journey to Selfhood

Book Theme

Analyzing character development

On her journey to Jo'burg and back, Naledi learns about her country—its geography, history, and social situation—as well as about herself. She learns about the Soweto uprising in 1976, when schoolchildren were murdered, and experiences the misery of a pass raid. She learns about her mother's difficult job away from home and the hard life of her people in the surrounding towns. She becomes aware of different ways to react to these injustices: There is Mma's quiet acceptance, Grace's outspokenness, and Dumi's participation in demonstrations and his decision to study abroad.

Naledi is a problem solver. During the course of her journey, she discovers new ways to respond to the injustices that she sees around her. In this activity, students look at three episodes on Naledi's journey to selfhood as she discovers what kind of action she can take. The activity focuses on Chapter 2, "The Road"; Chapter 6, "A New Friend"; and Chapter 15, "Hope." The chapters are short and can be read aloud or dramatized to refresh students' memories. For each chapter, have students summarize what happens and describe what Naledi learns about the kind of response that is possible. Discuss Naledi's insights and then have students write letters to Grace.

Suggested Answers

Chapter 2: What happens: Naledi and Tiro walk down a strange road singing songs. Naledi thinks about the pass and is afraid. Response: Older children make up songs to deal with their fear. (Some students may remember the anger of the boy in Chapter 8 who comes too late with his father's pass. "I'll burn this one day," he storms. That is another kind of response.) **Chapter 6:** What happens: The children learn about the segregated buses. They meet Grace Mbatha. Response: Her response to injustice is that she speaks her mind. She is not silent the way Mma is. "It's not you who should be sorry," she says. "Why shouldn't we use any bus?" **Chapter 15:** What happens: Naledi turns over in her mind the events of the last few days. She thinks about Grace and how Grace said things that made Naledi feel better: "We're pushed all over the place, but it won't be like that forever." She realizes that she cannot work things out all by herself. Response: She decides to write to Grace and to talk to other students. Students' letters will vary.

Inquiry Activity 5 • A Student's Account

Social Studies Theme

Comparing literary and firsthand accounts

When historical fiction is used to teach social studies, there is often a question of how accurately the author has described important events in history. Have events been dramatized or distorted for novelistic effect? Such questions are important to keep in mind for teachers and students alike. In exploring the social studies theme in *Journey to Jo'burg*, students have an opportunity to compare Beverley Naidoo's account of life in South Africa with excerpts from an interview with an African student who took part in the Soweto protest. The interview is from the Report of the Study Commission on U.S. Policy Toward Southern Africa *South Africa: Time Running Out*, (University of California Press, 1981). Students will find that the novel presents a remarkably accurate picture of life in South Africa in the 1980s.

Distribute Inquiry Activity 5 and have students work individually or in pairs to complete the chart. They will have little difficulty locating parallel episodes in the novel.

Discuss the similarities between the novel and the interview. You might point out how understated both accounts are. You can extend the activity by having students read other accounts of life in South Africa that parallel events in the novel.

Suggested Answers

1. Mma speaks of the parents' fear and suffering, Chapter 11. **2.** Grace's story, Chapter 10 **3.** the hospital episode, Chapter 12 **4.** Grace's story about her brother Dumi, Chapter 10 **5.** references to lanterns and Tiro's delight with the electric light; Naledi tells of buying water from the village tap, Chapter 10

Inquiry Activity 6 • A Fitting End

Social Studies Theme

Finding parallels between historical climate and the story's end

In light of the dramatic events that have followed the writing of *Journey to Jo'burg*, students consider how the mood at the end of the

Copyright © Sundance

novel fits the historical moment in which Beverley Naidoo wrote the story. Before students begin the activity, you may want to review briefly with them events that were taking place in South Africa in the mid 1980s. Explain that in the 1980s South Africa was undergoing many transformations. There was much political unrest and anger, and black and white people were beginning to change how they thought.

Suggested Answers

1. Students' answers will vary but should include some of the following. Naledi is saddened by her mother's return to Johannesburg. She wonders about Grace's words, "We're pushed all over the place, but it won't be like that forever." She thinks about Dumi and Grace's life trying to work and take care of all those boys. She worries about what she learns in school and how that might affect her dream of becoming a doctor. She thinks about people who have resisted the system of apartheid and wants to ask them about their choices. She is afraid of becoming a doctor but having little or no food and medicine to offer sick people.
2. Students' answers will vary but should focus on how Naledi's mixture of confusion, fear, and hope mirror the emotions black South Africans experienced in the 1980s. Naledi's choices—whether to work within the system like Mma or to oppose it like Dumi—correspond to real-life decisions many black South Africans faced during that time.

Inquiry Activity 7 • A Story for Freedom

Critical-Creative Thinking

Drawing inferences

Beverley Naidoo grew up in South Africa and moved to England when she was twenty-two years old. As a teacher, she looked for ways to make people aware of the problems in South Africa. She joined the Education Group of the British Defense and Aid Fund for Southern Africa (BDAFSA) and attended meetings where these problems were discussed. At one of those meetings, she got an idea. Why not write a story for young readers that explores some of the problems that South Africa faces? She could show people what it feels like to live in a country torn by racial strife, and she could offer directions for change. It would be her way of speaking out.

Beverley Naidoo wrote her book "In memory of two small children who died far away from

their mother . . . and to Mary, their Mma, who worked in Jo'burg." Perhaps she heard Mary's story at one of the meetings of the BDAFSA. Although the story that she wrote is not literally about a woman named Mary who lost two small children, there are references to this kind of tragedy in the book (the small grave Naledi sees in the village, the eight-year-old girl who died in Soweto, and the baby who died at the hospital). Through fiction, Beverley Naidoo found a way to let the world know about the suffering in South Africa.

In this activity, students analyze how effectively Beverley Naidoo's story addresses the goals of the BDAFSA, which have been "to help people who have been treated unjustly and to support their families and dependents"; "to bring attention to the racial problems of South Africa"; and "to help develop a nonracial, free society." Begin by reading aloud the section entitled "About the Author" at the back of the book. You might ask the class if they know of groups in this country with similar goals for other causes, for example, the NAACP, ACLU, or Amnesty International.

Talk with the class about what they learned about the problems in South Africa from reading *Journey to Jo'burg*. List students' answers on the chalkboard. Students may give such responses as Africans have to work away from their homes, they have to carry passes, their living conditions are poor, and schools teach only one point of view. Then list on the board some of the ways people in the story address these problems. For example, Grace speaks her mind, Dumi goes away to school, the boy whose father is taken away rages, Mma is silent, Naledi decides to talk to her friends. Distribute Inquiry Activity 7 and have students suggest how the book supports each of the BDAFSA's three goals.

Suggested Answers
Students' answers will vary.

Inquiry Activity 8 • Why Do We Care Now?

Critical-Creative Thinking

Recognizing the importance of the past

You may want to begin this activity with a discussion about what students feel they can learn from the past. Do they think the past has no effect on them? Or do they believe that the past influences who they are and the decisions

Copyright © Sundance

they make? To help students make connections, you may want to have them draw on their personal experiences: Did they have a particularly good or bad experience that changed the way they thought about themselves and others? You may want to share a story about your past and explain how it affects your life today.

In the activity, students discuss the importance of the memory of apartheid to black and white South Africans and to Americans. Students also choose an event in the American past that they think is important for people to learn about and to remember.

Suggested Answers
1. Students' responses will vary but should include ideas such as black South Africans need to remember the struggles and sacrifices their friends, relatives, and schoolmates made to protest apartheid. White South Africans need to be aware of the legacy of racial intolerance they inherit so that they can actively work against it and toward peace and understanding. Both groups need to remember the problems of the past so that they can prevent their country from ever returning to a system of apartheid. Remind students that, like the American Civil War or the Holocaust, apartheid will leave a lasting impression on those it affected. **2.** Students' choices of historical events will vary.

Inquiry Activity 9 • Singing Free

Writing

Writing poetry about freedom

In 1985, American singer and songwriter Paul Simon went to Johannesburg to work on his album *Graceland*. There he met Joseph Shabalala, the Zulu lead singer of the musical group Ladysmith Black Mambazo. Together they wrote the music for the album. *Graceland* became a hit, and Simon and the group toured the United States singing a message of freedom to packed concert halls. Back in South Africa, Ladysmith Black Mambazo sang twice a day to audiences in Cape Town. "It was our first time to sing in the hall to only white people like that," Joseph Shabalala recalls. His feeling about music? "It heals."

Paul Simon's imagination and the success of *Graceland* have highlighted a channel for political change—music and poetry. "These are the days of miracle and wonder," one song says. The release of Nelson Mandela in 1990 was a sign that things were finally changing. In this activity, students reflect on the climate of hope by writing their own poems about freedom.

After hearing Grace Mbatha's story about the Soweto uprising, Naledi thinks about "the word in big letters"—FREEDOM. "What did the word really mean?" she wonders. "Did it mean they could live with their mother? Did it mean they could go to secondary school?" Ask students what freedom means to them. Make a list on the chalkboard of all the places, moments, sounds, or moods that come to mind when students hear the word.

In *Journey to Jo'burg*, Naledi wonders, "So what would you learn in a school with freedom?" Explore the theme of freedom by having students discuss what a "school with freedom" means to them. The discussion may give students ideas for their poems. Tell students that their poems do not have to rhyme. They can repeat words as a refrain or use lines from the book.

Suggested Answers
Students' poems will vary.

Inquiry Activity 10 • The Next Act

Writing

Creating a play that finishes the stories in Journey to Jo'burg

In this activity, students write a class play that explores what might have happened after the book ends. Plays should include an act that takes place after apartheid has ended. You may want to divide the class into groups of three or four and have each group write an act. To make sure the acts follow logically, you may want the whole class to decide what generally happens in each act and then leave the writing to the individual groups. Before beginning to write, students should do some research on the situation in South Africa to make their play more authentic. Suggest that students use a narrator or other means to indicate time passing. Encourage students to perform their play for other classes in the school or for family members and friends.

Suggested Answers
Students should be encouraged to seek up-to-date data on South Africa. Reference sources from the local or school library or on CD Rom may be helpful.

Copyright © Sundance

Inquiry Activity 11 • Who's Who in South Africa

Project

Preparing biographical reports

Students will gain a better sense of events in South Africa if they have some knowledge of who the leading individuals on both sides of the apartheid conflict were. Divide the class into research groups, and have each group use library resources to prepare a short report on one individual.

The list of names for the research project includes these historical figures: **Cecil Rhodes,** powerful imperialistic governor of the Cape Colony in the late nineteenth century; **Jan C. Smuts,** long-time prime minister of South Africa up to the post-World War II years and an architect of the United Nations charter; **Alan Paton,** South Africa's greatest novelist, who appealed for racial understanding; **Pieter W. Botha,** prime minister from 1978 to 1989; **F. W. de Klerk,** elected in 1989, who dismantled apartheid legislation. There are four anti-apartheid leaders on the list: **Nelson Mandela,** a member of the African National Congress who was sentenced to life imprisonment in 1963 and was not released until 1990, and who became president in 1994; **Steve Biko,** a young African leader who died in prison in 1977, bringing worldwide attention to charges of police brutality; **Archbishop Desmond Tutu,** winner of the Nobel Peace Prize and an outspoken opponent of apartheid; and **Miriam Makeba,** a famous South African singer not allowed to return to her homeland because of her antiapartheid stance. Many of Makeba's albums are available and would be interesting for students to hear.

Suggested Answers

Students' reports will vary.

Inquiry Activity 12 • No Easy Answer

Making Connections

Students examine how poverty makes life very difficult for Naledi's family and for the majority of black South Africans. You may want to prepare students for the second question by reminding them that the dissolution of apartheid has not solved the enormous problem of poverty. There is still unequal access to educational and material resources between black and white South Africans. Students may want to consider how attitudes about racial differences linger even though the political system has changed.

Suggested Answers

1. The family's poverty makes it necessary for Mma to work many hours away from her children. There is also the implication that if they had other resources, Naledi's father would not have continued the dangerous work in the mine that gave him the coughing sickness. The family does not have enough money for nutritious food or for shoes. Much of the money is spent buying water from the village tap. To pay for the trip back home and to the hospital, Mma must borrow from others. **2.** Students' answers will vary.

Inquiry Activity 13 • Decisions

Making Connections

Analyzing opposing viewpoints and historical judgments

Most Americans were opposed to the policy of apartheid and felt a bond with the struggle of South Africa's blacks to end this oppressive system. But what could the people and the government of the United States do to help bring about change? This was a perplexing question, one that Americans debated for more than 25 years. An important aspect of the question was the role of United States business in South Africa. In the 1980s, pressure by citizens' groups in this country led many of the 350 American companies doing business in South Africa to pull out. Some business leaders insist it is better if their companies remain there. In this activity, students will weigh statements on both sides, enabling them to see just how thorny the issue was. Students will also consider what role protest has in correcting injustice.

Use the opposing viewpoints illustrated in this activity as the basis for a debate between two teams of students. Opinion in your classroom may be divided on the question of United States involvement. If so, that division accurately reflects the mood of the nation just prior to the end of apartheid. Extend the activity by having students discuss other methods of protest. You may want to focus on both international methods such as trade sanctions and on national methods of protest such as the sit-ins and marches used by African Americans during the civil rights movement.

Suggested Answers

Students' responses will vary.

Copyright © Sundance

Curriculum Tie-ins

LANGUAGE ARTS/SOCIAL STUDIES

In collections of African folklore, find folktales of the Zulu and other Bantu-speaking peoples of southern Africa to learn more about the values, customs, and beliefs of South Africa's black population.

LANGUAGE ARTS/SOCIAL STUDIES

Make a comparative study of the literature of the antiapartheid movement (see Suggested Reading) and the literature of black protest in the United States.

LANGUAGE ARTS/SOCIAL STUDIES

Another valuable comparative study can be made of literature about prejudice and discrimination in all countries. A good place to begin is the New American Library (Mentor Paperback) anthology *Prejudice*, a collection of 20 stories edited by Charles R. Larson (New York, 1971).

MUSIC

Students will enjoy and can learn from Paul Simon's popular album *Graceland*, which features the outstanding African singing group Ladysmith Black Mambazo. Simon has captured the rhythms and complex chord changes of African gospel music.

SOCIAL STUDIES

As a research assignment, have students use current news magazines to find out what is happening in South Africa today—how Mandela and others are trying to improve life for the majority of South Africans and what obstacles they face.

SOCIAL STUDIES

Divide the class into groups to prepare reports on different periods in the history of South Africa, such as the early Dutch settlements (1652–1832); British rule (1814–1910), the Great Trek and the creation of the two Boer republics (1832–1902), the discovery of gold and diamonds (1867–1887), the Boer War (1899–1902), and the development of modern South Africa (1910–present).

SOCIAL STUDIES

Have groups of students prepare collections of statements by individuals for the direction of the country in the future. Use these as the basis for a simulated conference between white and black South African leaders to see if differences can be resolved.

SOCIAL STUDIES

Examine the social, economic, and political life of South Africa today. Contrast the living conditions of whites with those of Africans, coloureds (people of mixed racial backgrounds), and Asians. The study should focus on how people live and what the prospects are for young people in each of the racial groups.

SPORTS

Interested students can find out the status of South African participation in international sports, especially how teams and individual athletes have been received in this country and elsewhere.

Copyright © Sundance

Bulletin Board

A display of "Life in South Africa" makes a good visual complement to *Journey to Jo'burg*. You can divide the board into three sections, with pictures about the Soweto uprising in 1976 on one side, pictures from political events today on the other, and pictures of everyday life in the middle. News magazines like *Time, U.S. News and World Report,* and *Newsweek* are good picture resources, as are *National Geographic* and *Life*. Ask students to bring in pictures that they find.

You might also choose to illustrate Tiro and Naledi's journey for a bulletin board display. Make a larger drawing of the map of their journey for the wall and have students work in groups to illustrate significant events. A border or frame around the pictures will make them look like snapshots. Place them where they belong on Naledi and Tiro's route.

To understand South Africa's strong economic base, you may want to create a map similar to the one below that shows the valuable minerals that make South Africa a resource rich country.

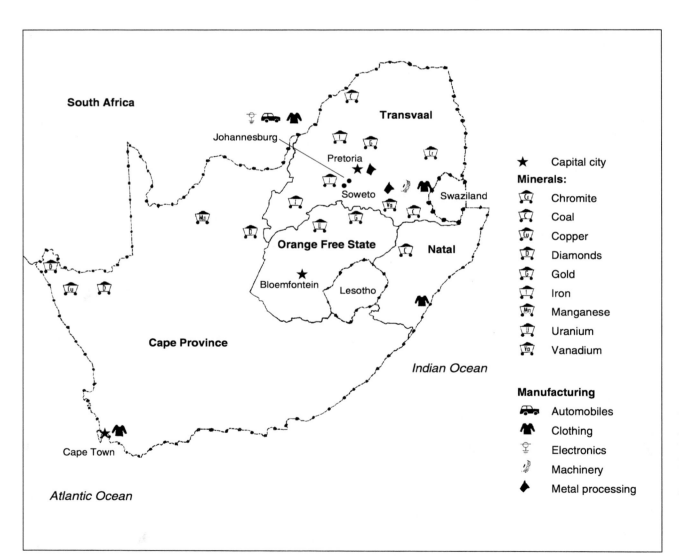

Copyright © Sundance

Suggested Reading

Books for Students

Bentley, Judith. *Archbishop Tutu of South Africa.* Enslow Publishers, 1988. Bentley presents a readable account of Tutu's life and his continuing crusade against apartheid. The narrative is intermixed with general history.

Lawson, Don. *South Africa.* Watts Publishing, 1986. This is a well-researched general history of South Africa and the evolution of apartheid.

Manning, Richard. *"They Cannot Kill Us All": An Eyewitness Account of South Africa Today.* Houghton Mifflin, 1987. The author is a journalist who was expelled from South Africa. He presents interviews with South Africans of varying viewpoints but with a strong antiapartheid message. The book contains some strong language.

Paton, Alan. *Cry the Beloved Country.* Random House, 1948. This classic novel is an appeal for interracial understanding, written by South Africa's leading author. It was published as apartheid was being made official government policy. The novel was made into a beautiful and moving musical called *Lost in the Stars.*

Books for Teachers

Brown, Godfrey N. *Apartheid: A Teacher's Guide.* UNESCO Press, 1981. A useful collection of 17 classroom activities providing a balanced approach to the issues. Teaching suggestions help students see how their lives are connected to events in South Africa.

Lelyveld, Joseph. *Move Your Shadow: South Africa, Black and White.* Penguin Books, 1986. This is New York Times reporter Lelyveld's Pulitzer Prizewinning account of apartheid in South Africa.

McCuen, Gary E. *The Apartheid Reader: Ideas in Conflict.* GEM Publications, 1986. McCuen has compiled a very good collection of primary sources, ranging from government statements to antiapartheid writings by Archbishop Tutu and Nelson Mandela. It also addresses the question of United States involvement in South Africa.

The Study Commission on U.S. Policy Toward Southern Africa. *South Africa: Time Running Out.* University of California Press, 1981. The early sections contain a detailed, authoritative, and remarkably readable account of South Africa's history and the policy of apartheid. Interspersed throughout are short selections called "South Africans Talking," which present all shades of opinion.

Audiovisual

Correspondents of the New York Times. *South Africa: Economics and Politics of Apartheid.* Random House Media, 1985. This sound filmstrip offers a good overview of the situation in the mid-1980s, with statements by government officials and by opponents of apartheid.

Copyright © Sundance

Notes

Copyright © Sundance

STUDY GUIDE 1

Journey to Jo'burg

This study guide covers Chapters 1–7.

To Think About as You Read

1. What dangers might Tiro and Naledi face on their way to Johannesburg?

2. How can you tell that Naledi and Tiro are very poor?

3. How do black South Africans help and protect each other?

Words to Look For

Mmangwane (Chapter 1)	pap (Chapter 3)	Rra (Chapter 4)
mielie (Chapter 3)	Tsamaya sentle (Chapter 3)	baas (Chapter 5)
Sala sentle (Chapter 3)	Tswana (Chapter 3)	Soweto (Chapter 6)

Questions for Discussion

1. How do Naledi and Tiro entertain themselves on their walk to Jo'burg? What would you do in their place?

2. How has their father's death made life harder for Naledi and Tiro?

3. In *Journey to Jo'burg*, what dangers do black South Africans face? Considering these problems, how do Naledi and Tiro show a great deal of courage?

4. Naledi notices that Grace is different from her mother. What seems to be the difference between the two women?

5. What differences do Naledi and Tiro see between the way they live in the village and the way people live in Jo'burg?

6. When Mma asks to take time off to see Dineo, how does Madam respond? What does Madam's response show about how she thinks of black people?

STUDY GUIDE 2

Journey to Jo'burg

This study guide covers Chapters 8–15.

To Think About as You Read

1. At the time *Journey to Jo'burg* was written, what dangers did black South Africans face every day in the cities?

2. How would you describe the feelings between black and white South Africans?

3. Think of Grace's story. What would you do if the government arrested one of your loved ones and you did not know for a long time where he or she was?

Words to Look For

raid (Chapter 8)	Hou jou bek (Chapter 8)	dustbins (Chapter 10)
pass (Chapter 8)	rubbish (Chapter 10)	queue (Chapter 12)

Questions for Discussion

1. What does Grace mean when she says, "Our people wash and clean up for others all day, but look how we must wash ourselves!"

2. Why do you think Grace uses the phrase "time of fire" to describe the events of the past?

3. Grace and Mma feel differently about the importance of school. What does each think about school?

4. Why do you think Grace's telling Naledi and Tiro about the schoolchildren's protests scared Mma?

5. Even though the medicine might make Dineo temporarily better, what problem remains unsolved at the end of the story?

6. What has *Journey to Jo'burg* made you think more about?

Copyright © Sundance

TIME LINE

Journey to Jo'burg

Read the paragraph below. Next, using information from the paragraph, find the dates for the five numbered events listed. Then enter each event and its date on the time line.

Naledi's story takes place about four years after the Soweto uprising of 1976. During the Soweto uprising, many young children were shot and killed by the police. A similar incident had happened before at Sharpeville in 1960. In 1980, the government began promising reforms. But, in 1989, there was still great unhappiness, and protest marches against apartheid continued.

1. Government promises reforms
2. The Soweto uprising
3. Sharpeville
4. Naledi's journey
5. Protest marches continue

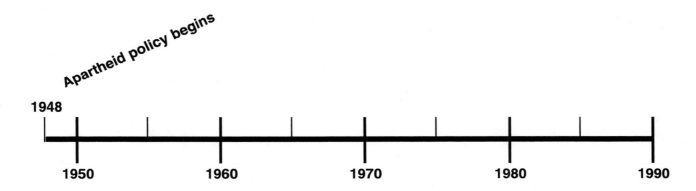

6. If you were to extend the time line to the present, what other events would you add? Explain briefly why you think these events are important to add to a historical time line.

Event/Year

Event/Year

Reasons:

Copyright © Sundance

MAP

Journey to Jo'burg

In South Africa during the time the story takes place, black Africans were assigned to live in areas called homelands and were not allowed to leave without a pass.

Use the map to answer the following questions.

1. What nations border South Africa?

2. What oceans border South Africa?

3. How many homelands were there? Count a divided homeland as one.

4. Which homelands were designated "independent"?

5. How many groups had more than one homeland area?

6. Compare the map with the one in the novel. What is the name of Naledi's homeland?

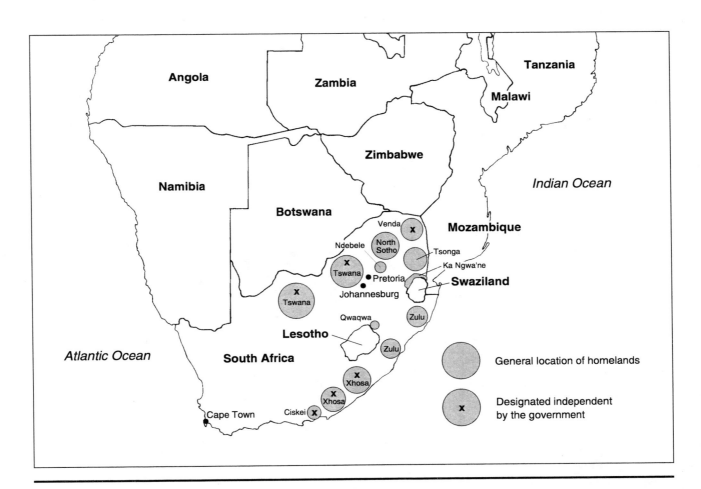

Copyright © Sundance

WHAT THE GOVERNMENT SAYS

Read the statements made by former officials of South Africa's government shown below. Then, in "Your Ideas," respond to them.

Government Statements

- "We must keep the Africans (blacks) separate to protect the purity of the white race."

- "The white man must rule, because he is elevated many, many steps above the black man."

- "A policeman may ask an African to produce his pass at any time. Failure to produce the pass on demand is a criminal offense punishable by a fine or imprisonment of up to three months."

Your Ideas

Imagine that you were a black teenager in South Africa in the 1980s. Based on the statements above, what do you think life would have been like for you? Write your ideas here.

Name _____

Copyright © Sundance

Inquiry Activity 1
CONNECT

THE SOUND OF ENGLISH

An idiom is a word or an expression that is commonly used by people who live in a particular place. British idioms differ from American idioms. Each of the underlined words below is British. Write what you think the word means. Then, after you have looked it up, rewrite the sentence using an American word.

1. "As the lorry sped on its way through the countryside, the children saw how the land was changing." (Chapter 4)

   What you think it means:

   Sentence with the American word:

2. "As the bus trundled along, stopping and starting with the traffic, there was a chance to stare out the windows." (Chapter 6)

   What you think it means:

   Sentence with the American word:

3. "On the banner that Dumi and his friends carried, they had written: BLACKS ARE NOT DUSTBINS." (Chapter 10)

   What you think it means:

   Sentence with the American word:

4. "Around the corner they found the queue of patients." (Chapter 12)

   What you think it means:

   Sentence with the American word:

GLOSSARY

Turn to the next-to-last page of the book to find the glossary. A glossary is a list of words and their definitions. In *Journey to Jo'burg*, the glossary contains South African words and expressions used in the story.

For each South African expression, write what you might say instead. For instance, instead of Rra, you might say "Dad" to your father and "Sir" to an elder.

Pap:

Sala sentle:

Mma:

Now imagine you are writing a story about your life for a South African student. Make a glossary of words or expressions you use that they might not understand. For instance, you might explain "What's up?" as a form of greeting like hello. You might explain french fries as strips of cooked potato.

　　　Inquiry Activity 3
Copyright © Sundance　　　　　　　　　　　　　　　　　　　**CONNECT**

JOURNEY TO SELFHOOD

At the end of the story, Naledi realizes that "through this journey she had begun to find out so much." One thing she learns about is the different ways people respond to troubling situations. For each chapter listed below, describe something important that happens and the different ways the people involved respond to these troubling situations.

	WHAT HAPPENS	**RESPONSE**
CHAPTER 2		
CHAPTER 6		
CHAPTER 15		

Imagine that you are Naledi. On another sheet of paper, write a letter to Grace Mbatha telling her what you have learned.

A STUDENT'S ACCOUNT

Journey to Jo'burg   **Social Studies Theme**

How accurate is *Journey to Jo'burg?* To find out, read the statements on this sheet; they are from an interview with an African girl who was a high school student in Soweto. For each statement, find a sentence or scene in the novel that sounds similar and write about it in the space provided.

FROM THE INTERVIEW	FROM THE NOVEL
1. "My parents were worried and afraid. They did not want me to go, because they said they did not want me to die."	
2. "I got the tear gas many times . . . Some of my friends were hurt and some died. One of my girlfriends was killed."	
3. "Sometimes my mother has to borrow from other people to make it through the month."	
4. "One of my brothers is in jail. We don't know why he is there. They will not tell us."	
5. "We have no electricity in our house. We have cold water from a tap outside the house."	

Name _____

Copyright © Sundance

A FITTING END

At the end of the story, Naledi is filled with thoughts and questions as she lies in bed.

1. Reread Chapter 15 and list five things that Naledi is concerned about.

2. How are Naledi's concerns for the future similar to the state of the country in the mid-1980s when Beverley Naidoo finished writing *Journey to Jo'burg?*

Copyright © Sundance

A STORY FOR FREEDOM

Journey to Jo'burg   **Critical-Creative Thinking**

Beverley Naidoo got the idea to write *Journey to Jo'burg* at a meeting of the British Defense and Aid Fund for Southern Africa (BDAFSA). The BDAFSA was created in 1958 to ease problems in South Africa and to bring about change. Complete the chart below. Explain how you think *Journey to Jo'burg* might have helped BDAFSA achieve three of its goals.

BDAFSA GOAL	WHAT DO YOU THINK?
1. To help people who have been treated unjustly	**1.** *Journey to Jo'burg* might have helped people who have been treated unjustly by
2. To bring attention to the racial problems of South Africa	**2.** The story brought attention to racial problems by
3. To help develop a non-racial, free society	**3.** The story might have helped create a free society in South Africa by

Copyright © Sundance

WHY DO WE CARE NOW?

Journey to Jo'burg   **Critical-Creative Thinking**

In the early 1990s, apartheid was abolished. In 1994, Nelson Mandela won the first democratic election in South African history and become president.

1. Despite the fact that the policy has changed, why do you think it is still important to study apartheid and to read books like *Journey to Jo'burg?* For each person listed, give reasons why that person should learn about apartheid.

A black South African student

A white South African student

An American student

2. Describe an event in the history of the United States that you believe is important for young people to learn about. Why is it important that people remember this event?

SINGING FREE

What does freedom mean to you? Write down the words—for places, moments, sounds, or moods—that come into your mind when you read the word freedom.

Now write a poem about freedom. Use the words you listed above for ideas. You may begin your poem with the words, "Freedom is . . . " or you may make up a different beginning. Decide if you want to repeat a line as a refrain.

THE NEXT ACT

There are many unfinished stories in *Journey to Jo'burg*. Imagine a part of the story that you would like to finish, such as what happened to Dumi after he was arrested, or what Naledi did when she went to school the next morning after returning home. Work with a group of classmates to write a play finishing one of the unfinished stories in *Journey to Jo'burg*.

You may want to begin your play where *Journey to Jo'burg* left off and have it end seven years after apartheid has been abolished. How might the characters' lives change during that time? How would you show these changes? Try to use some of the South African words and expressions found in the glossary. Brainstorm some ideas for your play in the space below. Use a separate sheet of paper on which to write your play.

WHO'S WHO IN SOUTH AFRICA

Journey to Jo'burg   **Project**

Use library resources to prepare a short report for the class on one of the individuals listed below. Your report should include basic information about the person's life, what he or she has said or done about race relations, what the person is best known for, and what influence he or she had on the struggle for freedom in South Africa.

Cecil Rhodes   Pieter W. Botha   Steve Biko
Jan C. Smuts   F. W. de Klerk   Archbishop Desmond Tutu
Alan Paton   Nelson Mandela   Miriam Makeba

Copyright © Sundance
                                                            CONNECT

NO EASY ANSWER

Many of Naledi's family's problems come from the fact that the family is so poor. For instance, Naledi and Tiro have to make the long journey to Johannesburg because they are too poor to afford a doctor in the village.

1. What other problems does poverty cause for the family?

2. Even though apartheid has now been abolished, what other problems will remain for many families in South Africa? List some problems and then brainstorm ways they could be solved. Share your ideas with your classmates.

Copyright © Sundance   **CONNECT**

DECISIONS

Journey to Jo'burg

Making Connections

In the 1980s, many American companies had offices in South Africa. At the time, there was a big debate in the United States about whether these companies should have left as a protest against apartheid or whether they did more good by staying. Read the arguments given by both sides. You may also want to do some additional research on this subject. Then write your opinion on another sheet of paper. Give reasons to support your opinion.

American Companies Should Leave

The American people and government must take a stand against apartheid. We are the nation people look to as the leader of freedom, democracy, and equality. If we stay, we are acting as if apartheid is all right. What kind of message does that send to South Africa's black people when so many black leaders have asked us to leave? If we leave, South Africa's economy will be hurt, and this may force the government to change.

American Companies Should Stay

American companies can try to improve wages and living conditions for Africans. We can build houses, schools, and hospitals. From a position within the country, we can let the government know how much we oppose apartheid. The blacks of South Africa will see that we care and want to help. If we leave, we cannot provide that help. In addition, we are such a small part of South Africa's economy that our departure will not hurt the white population. It will hurt the 70,000 blacks working for United States companies.

Besides American companies leaving South Africa, how else could the United States protest apartheid? How can people within a country resist or prevent unfair treatment by others?

Name _____

Copyright © Sundance

T 220504

	DATE DUE		